KINGFISHER READERS

level 2

Fur and Feathers

Claire Llewellyn

KINGFISHER

KINGFISHER

First published 2012 by Kingfisher
an imprint of Macmillan Children's Books
a division of Macmillan Publishers Limited
20 New Wharf Road, London N1 9RR
Basingstoke and Oxford
Associated companies throughout the world
www.panmacmillan.com

Series editor: Heather Morris
Literacy consultant: Hilary Horton

ISBN: 978-0-7534-3088-0
Copyright © Macmillan Publishers Ltd 2012

9 8 7 6 5 4 3 2 1

1TF/0512/WKT/UNTD/105MA

A CIP catalogue record for this book is available from the British Library.

Printed in China

Picture credits

The Publisher would like to thank the following for permission to reproduce their material. Every care has
been taken to trace copyright holders. However, if there have been unintentional omissions or failure to trace
copyright holders, we apologize and will, if informed, endeavour to make corrections in any future edition.
Top = t; Bottom = b; Centre = c; Left = l; Right = r
Cover Shutterstock/Richard Peterson; Pages 4 Shutterstock/Michael Pettigrew; 5t Shutterstock/Jeffrey
Van Daele; 5b Shutterstock/holbox; 6 Shutterstock/iDesign; 7t Shutterstock/FloridaStock;
7b Shutterstock/Studio 37; 8 Alamy/Wayne Hutchinson; 9 Photolibrary/OSF; 10-11 Photolibrary/Alaska
Stock; 11 Photolibrary/OSF; 12 Photolibrary/F1 online; 13 Photolibrary/Alaska Stock; 14 Frank Lane
Picture Agency (FLPA)/Mitsuaki Iwago/Minden; 15 Photolibrary/Bios; 16 Photolibrary/OSF; 17 FLPA/
Gerard Lacz; 18 Photolibrary/Bios; 19t Photolibrary/Animals Animals; 19b Photolibrary/Bios; 20 FLPA/B.
Borrrell Casals; 21t Photolibrary/OSF; 21b Photolibrary/Imagebroker; 22-23 Photolibrary/OSF; 24
Shutterstock/Eric Iselee; 25 Photolibrary/Peter Arnold; 26 FLPA/Konrad Wothe/Minden; 27 Photolibrary/
Aflo Foto Agency; 28-29 Photolibrary/OSF; 29 Photolibrary/Imagebroker; 30 Shutterstock/Pavel Losevsky;
31t Shutterstock/Alexander Gitlits; 31b Photolibrary/Whitez.

Contents

A coat of hair   4

A coat of feathers   6

Keeping warm   8

A fur coat   10

Keeping dry   12

A clean coat   14

Clean feathers   16

Growing fur   18

Growing feathers   20

A special coat   22

Look at me!   24

Hide and seek   26

Winter and summer coats   28

Coats for us   30

Glossary   32

A coat of hair

Dogs, cats and other **mammals** have hair that grows all over their body. The hair is thick and soft. It is called fur.

Sheep have thick, curly hair. It is called wool.

Humans are mammals, too. We have just a little hair. Can you see the hair on your body?

A coat of feathers

Birds have a coat of feathers.
Most birds have feathers
all over their bodies.

A tiny
hummingbird
has about
900 feathers.
Bigger birds have
many more.

A bird's feathers are not all the same. The feathers on the wings and tail are strong. They help the bird to fly.

Birds also have lots of tiny, fluffy feathers called **down**.

Keeping warm

Birds and mammals have warm bodies. They have to keep warm all the time. A coat of hair or feathers helps them do this.

Fur and down feathers lock in the body's heat. They trap air and keep it warm next to the body. They also keep cold air out.

A fur coat

Animals that live in really cold places need very warm coats.

Polar bears live in the **Arctic**. They hunt in the icy sea.

A polar bear's fur coat has two layers. Short, fluffy hairs next to the skin lock in the body's heat. Long, thick hairs over the top keep out the cold and wet.

Keeping dry

Ducks, swans and some other birds live in water. Their feathers are coated with oil. This keeps the birds dry.

Sea otters have such thick fur that the sea water cannot reach their skin. They feel warm and dry.

A clean coat

Fur coats get dirty and attract **pests** such as fleas. Mammals clean their coat by scratching or licking. This is called grooming.

Chimpanzees like to groom each other. They look for dirt in each other's fur and pick out pests with their teeth.

Clean feathers

Birds wash their feathers to get rid of dirt. They scrub them with dust to get rid of pests. Then they tidy them with their **beak**.

A bird's feathers last about a year.
After that they get old and worn.
One by one, they drop out and
new feathers grow.

Growing fur

Some mammals are born without
any fur. Hamsters are pink when
they are born. They have no fur
at all. They stay in their **nest** to
keep warm.

After five days, the hamsters' skin
gets darker and hair starts to grow.
After two weeks, their fur has
grown. Now they have a warm
coat and can leave the nest.

Growing feathers

Some baby birds have no feathers. Blue tits are pink when they **hatch**. They have no feathers at all. They stay in their nest to keep warm.

After five days, their feathers start to grow. After two weeks, the blue tits have all their feathers. Now they can leave the nest.

A special coat

A porcupine's coat is made of hair, but it also has a lot of sharp spines. The spines grow up to 12 centimetres long.

Most of the time, the spines lie flat. They stand up if the porcupine is in danger. The porcupine can use its spines to hurt an attacker.

Look at me!

Peacocks have long tail feathers. They show them off when they are looking for a **mate**. They lift them and shake them loudly.

Male lions have thick, furry **manes**. The lion with the longest mane looks bigger and stronger than all the others. This helps him to find a mate.

Hide and seek

Some animals have coats that help them to hide.

A weasel has a brown coat, which blends in with leaves on the ground. This makes it hard to see.

Owls hunt at night. In the daytime
they sleep in trees. Their feathers
blend in with the **bark** and make
them hard to see.

Winter and summer coats

Some animals have a winter coat and a summer coat.

The Arctic fox has a winter coat of thick white fur. This keeps it warm and hides it in the snow.

In summer, the snow melts. The Arctic fox grows a new brown coat to hide it on the ground.

Coats for us

Humans have hair, but it does not keep us warm or dry. We need to wear clothes. We make some clothes from the coats of animals.

Sheep have a warm woolly coat. We use it to make woolly hats, scarves and gloves.

How do we keep dry? We copy ducks and swans and make our own waterproof clothes!

Glossary

Arctic a very cold part of the world in the far north

bark the outside of a tree trunk

beak the hard mouth of a bird

down small, soft, fluffy feathers

hatch to break out of an egg

mammal an animal that gives birth to its babies and feeds them on milk

mane the long hair on the head of an adult male lion

mate the partner that an animal has babies with

nest the place where an animal has its babies

pest a small animal that harms or bothers other animals